MUSKETS FOR THE BEAR PROBLEM

Muskets for the Bear Problem
© Andrew Whitmer / Cathexis Northwest Press

No part of this book may be reproduced without written permission
of the publisher or author, except in reviews and articles.

First Printing: 2024

ISBN: 978-1-952869-89-1

Cover art by C. M. Tollefson
Designed and edited by C. M. Tollefson

Cathexis Northwest Press
cathexisnorthwestpress.com

MUSKETS FOR THE BEAR PROBLEM

*Poems by
Andrew Whitmer*

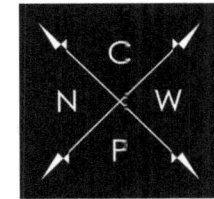

Cathexis Northwest Press

for marissa, right into the shadow

broad streets of fire, and leaping flames, blazed at many points
their brightglow emphasized by the darkness of night

pliny the younger
witness to the eruption of mount vesuvius

TABLE OF CONTENTS

invasion of the orange grove	1
henrietta broken	3
the pig loves it	4
did mary have her baby?	6
great serpent mound	7
bear flag republic	8
a few tears over roadkill	10
conscription for the bear problem	11
kalahari rumspringa	13
virtue signaling in pigtown	15
nap in the shade of a douglas fir	16
pacific northwest totem pole	17
paradise material	19
the tiger people	21
the bear problem	23
for the director of music	25
sherman's march to the sacramento kings	27
compound fracture	29
the living dead buffalo	30
jeannie needs a shooter	31
chimp sixty-five	33
adrenochrome bacchanalia	35
joy in mudville	37
tree in the rain	38
deception pass	40
constellations of the south	42
mountain in the western sky	44
square peg, square hole	45
teach grandpa to suck the eggs	47
harmonica roads	49
muskets for the bear problem	51
the moon is orange	53

INVASION OF THE ORANGE GROVE

years were negotiated for oranges
oranges and other people
in the open grove, in the open heat
open wounds were now colliding with spaceships

and the open wife was gone
she took a bad car swerving around citrus county florida
over a problem with the exhaust system, it kept a little boy waiting, and wondering
how long it might take to buy cigarettes

whereas prior to the spaceships, this was a rectangular life
it chewed on the dust, it hissed, and it metastasized
it heaved the hot air, while the heel bones banged into rocks
the wife, in monologues, threatened to kill herself for a while, until she didn't
until the fight she had left grew wings, told the farmer to fuck himself
and packed-up all her wigs

but then this morning, in an unrelated surprise
the aliens were here, they arrived tapping a public address system: is this thing on?
tottering, the earth gave death a mixed response, you can imagine
the naked futility, how it made the farmer miss her tiredness, his wife
and the deliberate tension, as both bigger and darker shadows were now creeping over the farm
he missed everything, this was humbug
apologizing, and bargaining with palm leaves in the sand

so it goes, for the grove was already browning, unbecoming in a matter of hours
as blackness overtook the prized seminole pumpkins
the farmer tried to allow himself to feel, to make of time an understandable crawl
to focus in the intense way that a person sometimes can, the goldenrod overlook
not easily found, and then fortified

under cannonfire, a quiet throb choked on the spine, at the base of the neck
polaroids of a moonlit woman calcified, a climb into a green car
an echo that rolled away, the undreamed crunch of death on driveway stone
comprehended, and accepted, it fostered an indifference to the aliens, and a habit of swaying

without thought, this was when the farmer found himself wondering, inquiring
if the boy, if his wonderful son
wanted to blissfully draw on his bedroom wall, and so he asked him: what do you think?
it was a prompt about the dinosaurs
it was a hiccup in the spirit of limited time

because yesterday the answer was no, but today the spaceships were real
and he had always marveled at the boy, it was remarkable, how he memorized the hurricanes
with dust in his teeth, with the joy he found in a worn-out crayon

HENRIETTA BROKEN

henrietta was gulping down wine from a pringles can, for this was the catalyst
of unknown dogs, drooling over a trail of broken potato chips, who kept pace
with her electric scooter, there in the morning freshness of an asphalt parking lot
whereupon she gargled the purple merlot, as if it were purple mouthwash
and then rocket-fired her snot at the ground twice
resolved, as she rolled into that store on the wheels of a dream, buzzing
she took the beef, she took the texas corn salsa, henrietta took five sudokus
as quick as a flash, she laughed and then took the last can of who hash
it was because she needed to need
she needed to want to achieve a specific outcome
but henrietta made such poor, dog-loud use of that buzzing scooter, that she fell-over sharting
with a laugh, and snorting like a javelina boar, as both she and the jeanrack timbered
gracelessly, she belched from the ground, and then she pulled out a knife, hey
hey, hey, she said, you know what?
she stabbed into the air the story of an invisible sister, waiting in the parking lot, alone
she said, hey, she said, on and on like that: fuck yourselves, give me a hand, etc, etc
so she is, regrettably, no longer welcome at the wichita falls location, this is understandable
that her creaky bones must now lubricate at home, or scoot into a cracker barrel
whereupon she can lean into an elbow, rest the weight of a cheekbone onto a buttered biscuit
and see how long she can balance a packet of jelly on the side of her nose, brainstorming
because what kind of gun lets you roll out of a radioshack towing something big?
she's asking for a friend, a family member
a person who is in there trying to remember something, and that something is kaleidoscopic
it is henrietta's natural henrietta, uninterrupted, and unbroken
she is trying to remember the person she wants to believe in
the person who still believes in radioshack
it keeps her going places, it keeps her looking for Jesus in all of the mistakes
that was the gist of all the belching earlier, of all those hiccuped explanations
about the sister who waits, for a very long time
a life was trying to get started again, and she felt like she had been extremely clear
about the soul of it all, about the emergency that made her take things, she wanted to get away
with a new life in the name of redemption, this was the breakthrough
that would put her back together again, for the first time, on a day reserved for fate's perfection
she was stealing, and she was standing upright, googly-eyed and gratified
with the journey, because nobody just wakes up like that one day, all-foamin' at the mouth
jonesing to hold a knife to a manakin's throat, please
she is not fucking crazy, she is midwestern
there is no manakin law against that, again, all of this was explained, over and over
how badly she needed those things, what-with time being a constant
and therefore change being a certainty, death was everywhere, and she could smell it
the garlic descent, the parmesan encroachment, she could hear it
the sound of the corn growing, the sound of the corn growing, the sound of the corn growing
all of this was explained, and she kept on saying it
so what part did security not understand? and why all of the flashing lights?

4
THE PIG LOVES IT

down where it's lost, brazen, and pacing in the slop
mud between its molars, draped in caramelized onions, it wants you to take your clothes off
sigh, and then cannonball, do it
bring your worst, it sends word
bring that weak shit right back down here
and start remembering the good times, here's an old coupon
still good for one lit firecracker, for one little push down one little chipmunk's one little throat
foretold, being told, to do yourself a favor
and go throw that thing into a passing car's open window, good susan
the relief, another john wayne shell casing, you are welcome
for the crimson tide, rolling in the undercurrent of the physically dominant gender
which is buckshot, a valley of trouble, you know what it is
it is a fire quenched in saliva until the story crumbles into a dental record, forgotten
underneath the birds of drool, and their shadows
wings high above the mixed wine drying in the desert, circling
and screeching over a sundial, which is being wrong, and then staying wrong
a snow angel you can make, in the bed that you made
out of peanut shells, corn husks, fingernails, and rabbits feet
little packets of mustard, torn empty in barbeque smoke
when everybody's favorite song comes on the radio, is a knob they can play with
something they can poke with a finger
a wheelchair they can push out in front of a chicken truck
ahead of a slow afternoon's passing over femur bones, and old teeth
plastic eyes, googly formations under formations of cloud, googled
and glued, to the top of an open spine, hate me, beauregard in the hour he is made to lie down
in the slavery of dry-boned silence
mouthing to the empty heat well-rehearsed apologies, undeliverable to festering wounds
and just thinking about everything for a good, long, never-ending while
open ribs in an open grave
where a story remains closed, and you will never be able to make things right
so you will not object
when birds do what birds do, when time is as it ever was
you will eat your own hands, a perpetual sighing over perpetual failure
to realize, in very real time, that the journey was your sole entitlement
until you got to where you were going, it was your lone possession
and now all that remains is a hole in the mud, one that empties itself daily

just so it can fill itself up again, one memory at a time
just so it can all disappear
with each passing hour, the specifics of a soul's natural shine
counted, remembered, waved goodbye and then counted and remembered again tomorrow
the sting of today, and tomorrow's tomorrow, without any possible meaning beyond the pain
because there are no mysteries left to crochet, or even paint by number
no more questions, and no more color
which is everything, and then some, lost to the event horizon

DID MARY HAVE HER BABY?

mary screams at the constellations
high above the folsom bridge, on the banks of the little river
and on page forty-two of your textbooks, she screams her upside down little head off
is what she does, gasoline and meat, that's what she is, mary is a problem
an insect, the current moment's incendiary representation of an infestation
that insists, and persists unapologetically stealing the air, that fucking grasshopper
got so mad yesterday, so lost in outer space concerning the fate of her husband
that they basted her with motor oil, the little thief, over the river and through the woods
over the branch they threw a rope, skillfully, over an overdue apology, it is asking nicely
it has her by the ankles, it has a bird's eye view of a soul's attempt at escaping its proxy
while it burns in ceremony, while tippy-toed onlookers with their guns cocked
bob-around from behind each other's shoulders
and smoke settles into the soft hairs of their forearms, and their eyelashes, opening and closing
like blinds over the windows to an alleged soul, unmoved by the screaming, by the heat
of the flames, now that they can see better, now that they can appropriately sniffle, tilt their heads
and think clearly, and focus intently, this is how they chose to spend their evening, with a hobby
a purpose found in pointing torch fire at otherized human muscle, observed, and overheard
when in the middle horrors of an uneven cook, came the punctuation of moonshine comments
lines worth remembering later when the wife wants to know how everything went
questions asked over a cooling pie, questions asked about the cooling child
about the potential energy they saw flickering in the firelight, a viability behind a belly button
that could not be missed, not once time, marching forward, instructed her adult bones
to poke through her charred american skin, molten and crispening
in the nighttime breeze of may
when her unborn child, next in the bugline, was sawed with conviction from her open guts
under the terror of her open eyes, this fact unfolded
and you can read that again, because that is what they did, the execution of a pro-life agenda
recollected, that a baby was allowed just two coughs of brooks county air
one welcome to georgia, in that molasses drawl, and a singular come back and see us real soon
contemplated, that all eight of its life-having months were stomped into the dirt
stomped as if it were an eggplant that had done something to offend a bootheel
so one terrible thing swung and counted time over the other, dripping
as mary bled-out screaming, in the torchlight at unbothered smiles, at the baseball fans
who marked her grave with an empty bottle of sour mash
having dropped inside of it a lit cigar, which, like mary, burned until it didn't
under the stars that looked away, and on page forty-three of your textbooks
whereupon they unloaded into her american corpse, over one hundred american bullets, selah
because there is always a next page, always-always a next page, it is adorable
our unshared love for all those classic sunrises, because the short answer here is no
mary did not have her baby, and that is a conversation, meant for a capital one commercial break
for a little bit of imperialist side-chatter, over a burger with american cheese
with bubbles from an american beer, during this year's iron bowl, say terrible things out loud

GREAT SERPENT MOUND

vietnamese pigs were snoring in the slop, pot-bellied as a matter of biology
underneath a moonless, southern ohio presentation of orion
meaning the stars were at their brightest, they were celestial when the big family lined-up
the neighbors and took the color from their eyes, with hollow points, left estuaries running
from the holes in their skulls, the blood crept through the barn dirt, like black lava
after familial coffee at the kitchen table, where together they had made the silencers
brass-catchers from the wal-mart kept the shells off the floor, and the feds away
but life still had to pause, in stillness and in anger, and for a while, in bitterness
it stopped, it stared out into the gulf of alaska, marinating with intention
and then it started-up again
no more chinese takeout, no more pointing at the orcas and talking about someday
because they turned all the lights back on, worked the grooves back into the couch cushions
and went to the grocery store just to make eye contact, the same with church
and from the banks of the ohio river at sunset, they whispered over to kentucky
all of their quiet baptist secrets, which hovered over the water like clouds of rain
drizzling new details into the faces of all those limp shoes
a picture that hangs in every room
the time that this happened, the time that that happened
your own little frozen part in the frozen dirt turning a warm personality into a frozen skull
except for this time, she said, zero shovels for the bullshit neighbors
this per a direct instruction
one that grandma was pretty damn clear about, wanting them left as they were, neatly
there in a row, it was a whole lecture on symmetry, a family chat concerning aesthetic
because how else were the photographers going to take the right pictures?
wondering out loud, she pantomimed her lost expression
like a culturally-appropriated chimpanzee, over a burning cigarette and a hopewell ashtray
she wore these little miami earrings, a set she made from bird bone, and turquoise
having shot the bird herself, having ripped it to shreds over a patsy cline song
which was crazy, but why should they let themselves worry?
just let them take the fucking pictures
because everybody needs to remember, don't let anybody forget which flag waves the highest
she explained, and, more importantly, which flag has waved the longest
so only the pigs are going to squeal, does everyone understand?
those are all still posted, and poised for sale, the pigs
absolutely we are taking calls
is that a real question? what's changed? we do our job
twenty grand a pig, and that's just business, the business of vigilante justice
which is a shinier thing to call it, of course, all of it
the stuff we don't know about, never heard of them, don't know what you're talking about
go fuck yourself, you and you and you
multiplied, all of you, you and all of your structures of crumbling trust
please do something about it
who around here do you think teaches sunday school?
who has something they would like to say?

8
BEAR FLAG REPUBLIC

    the government stole the black hills from the lakota tribe
    that is the story, more or less, of the san francisco chronicle
    of how the california grizzly died as a captive in golden gate park
    a cold paw hanging from the bars of its cell, a paw that landed in a heavy thud
    when monarch the golden bear was finally granted his spiritual pasture, long may he roam
    in a warm death, limber and loose, because two very stiff decades had come and gone
    since the enormous grizzly was duped, hustled onto a train with mutton and honey
    since he was stolen to sell newspapers, to frown, to sit still
    in confinement, to daydream through tears over the lost california coastline, a golden childhood
    and its fishbone saturdays, the naps, taken on rocks in the sun, snoring to the sound
    of the ocean waves crashing, and then he woke up one morning to a job working in print media
    sulfur in the air and nowhere to roam, nothing to protect, sighing over the noise of
    garbage trucks, the bear could no longer hear the ocean and its waves, he could no longer feel
    the value of his own life, so the gentle monarch huffed through broken smiles at the flowers
    carried by small children, he cried and cried, sniffling for long hours after everyone
    retreated homeward, it was a death before death, which is the wild without its wilderness
    lost color, what betrayal does to a soul
    when sometimes, sometimes it really is possible to be so sad about something
    that you hope the tears never stop, because joy would just feel so unnatural, and wrong forever
    because there is a public domain picture of monarch, his snout poking through the steel
    little eyes are open, but you can tell, he is no longer trying to see a thing
    that all of his light is gone
    and that love, the basic warmth of life, he no longer believed it would ever return, and it didn't
    so now, out in the mojave desert, out there in the heat of its rattle
    the thought occurs that ten steps taken in any direction means california might kill you
    because california should kill you
    pick a reason, maybe the one about the two hunters who shot a cub by accident
    hid in a hole, and unfortunately survived
    spent the night listening to a mother's roaring grief, and her baby's wailing at the orange moon
    they told the newspapers all about it, said next time they would be up in a tree stand
    because we all know what sells, one page after another about shooting our problems in the head
    monarch's ancestors, for example, were poisoned with strychnine pesticides
    chemicals loaded into pig entrails, hung from trees
    as shackled bears were made to fight with goring bulls, in the dust, and tequila sweat
    resolved, they were skinned into chairs for andrew jackson, and then they were sat on
    the monarch himself was stuffed, and put behind glass, like a corpse might make a run for it
    like the dead can't hold a pose long enough to be remembered on the state flag

the golden state, golden, and shining onward, okay
all of the natives, and all of the california grizzlies, golden, are gone, not okay
shot dead just for breathing, eureka
the bull swings up, the bear swings down, and history is an octopus
so taxidermy monarch wants the fourth graders, breathing into the plexiglass, to pay attention
he says history is an octopus, kids, your parents use moral codes to protect tax codes
certainly not you, hopefully your fate isn't taxidermied, just for going to school
just for wanting to think about the mountains, and the mystery, how the ocean never ends

A FEW TEARS OVER ROADKILL

there is not one piccolo trumpet, wrote the incarcerated paul
zero are silver, waiting and hoping, reserved
to mark your luminous anger
nope, not with any kind of special, pink-lit chorus
not in the way you would have it
no french horns will be played in remembrance
somber, or polished, no muckduck will be given
not one trombone made ready
or prepared, to fart along
to your mincemeat, to your turquoise frustration
this, what?
to the tune of the holy saints? and the holy-inward march?
when the unicorn, which was thy truest gift
is now a cart mule?
a wheezing never-was?
that which is no longer suited for field jerky? or even pig slop?
no, jeremy
you were told, denise
it will go to the wolves
and you will go to the wolves
because trees fall in silence all the time

CONSCRIPTION FOR THE BEAR PROBLEM

to be posted immediately

whereas attention to the public good has been called
notice and abide, by order of settled law
those citizens to which the following voluntarily applies, please, notice and abide
in accordance with addendum XV to the town charter, and effective immediately

to whom it so clearly concerns

please, form your best possible line at fire station number three please,
expect to be greeted peacefully, so long as you are peaceful

we are very aware, of course we are aware, of your collective status
ongoing, organized, the jorts, all per your flyers
we do get it
we had no other choice, but to get it

one flintlock musket, per our loud discussion
the terms of your banishment, as was loudly discussed
are now available, again, at fire station number three

to be clear, and official
absolutely all canaries
are hereby invited to leave the coalmine
please exit the town, resolved

please feel encouraged, do something about your issue
now yours to own privately, and in-accordance with settled law
that which you shriek from the corners of our bars
the sidewalk that never ends, please
box your glacier elsewhere

we agree with your premise entirely, and support you completely, in your departure
the hopes and prayers of liberty-loving people everywhere march with you

therefore, in plain language
know that the promised hour of mobilization is upon you
the great crusade you have been hallucinating
awaits finally, it finally awaits
the eyes of the world are upon you
your drivers, we made sure of it, have all been paid and tipped
please, please leave
thank you, and congratulations

KALAHARI RUMSPRINGA

warm and fluffy towels, on white, rubber-plastic lounge chairs, are waiting for the amish
by the navy blue indoor pool, by the green and purple tube slides, gushing
with retreated sewer water, and top forty radio
where the amish should note the oversized t-shirts worn by the men
wading in the urine, a status from whence parenthood imagines the appetizer sampler plate
at the bennigan's opposite the splash pad, human pamplona virus and you, amish
what to know, and welcome to earth
the kingdom of neon-lit negotiation, we want you to try the mozzarella sticks
once everyone has showered-away from themselves the hot tub generalities
once seated, once tucked, then you lay the cloth napkin across your denim lap, amish
there is a cold, black and orange drink machine at the liquorice bar
the waterslide waits for you
glowing, and ready to serve from three bottles of jagermeister at the same time
because it is likely the need will be there, because everyone else will be there, believing
with loins quivering with crockpot alfredo, what do you think?
is this number of restaurants to choose from not heaven itself?
the water is warm, and it says chlorinated things, it shoots lines of blood into the eyes
with big new perspectives, everywhere you look, another television and a new dream
the disney bundle, the childhood you never had, so incredibly sad, so let us take your hat
so that you can take a seat, tell us about your horses, but don't you have a tractor?
haven't you always wanted to pump that big amish cock of yours, satisfied
stomach full of potato skins, loaded
into one of these bonnetless, big-titted beauties? one of these beatrices
always speeding past your buggy, hairs flowing in the breeze?
remember to pronounce the l-sounds in the word quesacilla phonetically, amish
order yourselves a cosmopolitan, never say excuse me, and you will fit right in
which is everything you ever wanted, or needed
that is us, everyone else, and you are so welcome for that
for the sushi served warm under the neon lights
that is what it means to rest, because we also sell neck pillows, vape pens, buffalo sixty-nine
and warming gel, here in the hotel gift shop, would you care for some lemon water?
or a five hour energy drink? thank you for choosing us, amish
as we know you had choices to make, and honestly, that sounds exhausting
so how many nights will you be staying? let's get you out of the sunshine, you poor things
let's get you kind folks into a couple of these plush bathrobes, and sandals
always sandals, because watch where you step, and again welcome
again you are so welcome, please report any unresolved carpet stains to your server

or a migrant worker avoiding eye contact, thank you so much
for you have entrusted to us the very first day of the rest of your lives
so we will clean the carpet, if you just let us know, we will address whatever you might find
because whatever the world means to you, your money means the world to us
and this is a house built on unshakeable gratitude, come whatever might come
wherever that might happen, to us it is the end of a rainbow, to us you carry a shine
please let us get that for you, please let us understand, for the moon is rising
and we can help, because they get paid to clean that up, so they know they have to do it

VIRTUE SIGNALING IN PIGTOWN

the bright orange baltimore oriole
humble, in its diamond crown fedora, thank you so much
it has nothing more to say about the boring, and unbearable
baltimore raven, nothing more, that is, than the baltimore raven
hasn't already said about its bullshit, baltimore self
it is an air guitarist, more like the telltale *fart*, thank you, do you quarrel?
that lexicon of litter, that avian mange
that is *not* an attractive bird
it is bad animalia, but of course, always
keeping that same energy, rest assured
always a bit louder for the people in the back, goodness grief, it's giving
the dullness of a baby dill pickle
floating by itself in cold vinegar
it is a pollutant, lazily tapping the bubbled-up nevermores
of a dull-eyed fetus, calling to the surface of its glass jar
and popping there in a stink, nobody cares!
a vimless yawn! a broken twat! the raven sucks!
it does not mist itself with bleu de chanel, by chanel, one hundred and eighty-five dollars
it collects dust, this bird
it breathes the bloated squawking of its stolen colors
selfishly held to both create, and to better-know
the baltimore darkness
this being the alleged sole mystery with which a baltimore bird should even baltimore bother
nonsense, humbug, you stole, and now you look like afterbirth
because you are, and always will be, evermore and you know it
that no one could ever love you
but this is only a notion, nothing more and nevermore
be your own meadowlark, do you quarrel?
do you quarrel at the drop of a small bird's little brown hat?
to close, and to the notion: au revoir! au fuck you so much!
your mother!
your mother *wishes* that she had these orange feathers, *wishes*

NAP IN THE SHADE OF A DOUGLAS FIR

a magnificent red apple, it has a seedy little core
for it is littered
absent-mindedly, imagining ants and squirrels, and the birds of april
wishing it was bright green, the apple
in a breezy, and explainable, okay universe
in which a cold yellow popsicle
is under a tree, on the blue picnic blanket of an unbothered summer
a nap is softening in the forest lawn
in the smell of its grass, in the streaks of its light
the buzz of a bee then lands on a purple flower
and it does nothing, in cinematic frame
it is all peach cobbler
breezy, and effortless
as the wind is cautiously able to carry time, featherly, now and then
conversely, should a tree fall in the woods
the brown bear will indeed hear it, or in this case smell it
the red apple core, the yellow popsicle wrapper
the peach cobbler in the open tupperware
snoozing, and dreaming
what is the twilight future?
an object no longer in motion
her french braid, it will come to a rolling stop
next to a wet log
and bugs will call it home

PACIFIC NORTHWEST TOTEM POLE

in the aquamarine inlets off washington's tall tree shores
gliding through the shadows of our flyaway trident missiles, and the olympic mountains
meandering, the black and white orcas, and the humpback whales
play together an ensemble of ancient, cold water hymns
transforming the sea into a pink mist, crawling its way under the trees
slowly to the overture, to the port orchard patriarchy, they know it so well, they are humming
and unworried, dutiful to the flowers of generational hillside gardens, cold rainier cherries
colder worries about the seahawks, on porch swings in the breeze, the music is easy to hear
but this same whale-born hymn, it is also heard faintly by the baseball drunks marooned
in the peninsula's douglas firs and fainting, in its pinecone parking lots, leaning over baskets
of loser pull-tabs in belfair, in bremerton, in the dive bars of the winding altitude roads
they are praying to the neon signs
in consideration of the ferris wheel rider, the lost millennial high above the pike place market
downtown, over the puget sound's babbling water, and the nuclear submarines
a nobody can hear the music, the same as it ever was, humming to forget
about a life spent lost between volcanoes, the grind of a sawmill, and unacted upon dreams
concerning the stripper who makes his coffee, consistent through the winter
in the little shed by the gas station where he also buys his marijuana, he sighs and he wonders
if the supersonics will ever return paddling a canoe, and yearning with unbroken resolve
when a beluga whale below him cuts through the city's carnival lights, laughing, and also crying
as the colors of the northern air waft-around like sheet music, this is direction
for the sound a whale can make with the personality hidden in its smile
there, in one of the few places left on the planet that can still feel like home
this is all bad noise, malarky to the fellowship of wet boxes shivering by the interstate
to the pile of people by the football stadium, a collective of burning cigarettes
shoulder to shoulder, and yelling over the airplane engines
about the bald eagle they think they saw today, about the life they keep in their pockets
the buttons, and the lint, the inventory of dying alone, listed
and endured by the undead, the puyallup tribe sweating in red polyester
and trying to hear themselves think in the smoking section of a carpeted casino
with grease stuck to their faces, with cotton candy stuck in their hair
the mountain has been lost
there is nothing spiritual concerning the slack-jawed pauses taken by the gift shop totem poles
it is such a shame, such a shortcoming of expectation
how there are no canoes left to polish, or better days ahead
how time will never again shine out in the distance
and sparkle with a greatness foretold, not so much, but bill over there

is thinking about leasing a fucking corolla, beyond that, nothing waits over the horizon
or is wondered about at all, not in the sadness
of the artificial lighting, or the desperation of the ventilated air, the unkept time
absolutely not, the eagles they surrendered are never coming back
so prayer only flickers like a kicked habit, you just empty the ashtrays
and talk to the police, vacuum over the tinnitus, a train without a caboose, lost, with no hope left
not even for a passing thought, that of a pleasant bird, remembered above the rising smoke
and nesting, in the shadows of a canaanite parking deck, found, forgotten, again fucked again

PARADISE MATERIAL

there is such a thing as hopelessness

they are saying, life turned sentence that trails off

a failure, yeah, yeah, yeah

texas roadhouse

ad infinitum, pump up the jam

all of that bread

for a fraction of people, chewing above the pie

for dessert, for the gram

sauce bouncing off white robes

that makes sense, it does, it was their idea

to design themselves, to live, to receive the outcome

more butter is needed for the table

bar napkins and three orange whips

so it goes

and the band played on

the band played september, for it was the sunshine band

sunshine, they said, bright rays forever and ever

for us, good old us

at the block rate hotel, towels on demand

for good old us, far out of earshot

and miles over brimstone, please, not another drink

just the last one again, ice it to the brim, that guy will say

and her, and them, all those lotioning under a specific consideration

THE TIGER PEOPLE

after many tropical centuries of continual disinterest, with any and all civilization
and whatever it might be doing, or perfecting, destroying in all directions
beyond the oceanic horizon, far past the island's concern
the passing years vociferously established that coconuts exclusively, exclusively coconuts
could be used to construct passing goodwill, to all men, to those who would otherwise greet
intrusion with a most violent hostility, incendiary, and without exception, always
since forever, as it was annotated, marco polo having declared them a most brutish
and savage race, with heads, eyes, and teeth like those of dogs, an intensely cruel people
marco polo said, that would kill and eat every foreigner upon whom they could lay their hands
that attitude remains, for it is a watchtower, it is very much awake for the boats that wander
too close to private property, in the middle of the indian ocean, the guaranteed expectation
should be an all-consuming anger, and flying arrows
the arrows that greeted the helicopter pilot, tasked to check on their well being
after the big tsunami, and despite the language, which no linguist can break, please fuck off
speaks plainly enough in other ways, we will kill you
and your entire family, that is definitely the message when you give someone a pig
and a couple of dolls, and then that someone decapitates them promptly, and in quick succession
resolved, they make sure that you are watching
while they bury it all on the beach, shouting what you presume to be expletives, for sure
that volume, as more arrows, cocked and loaded, are released to test the distance
you might even have a waterproof bible, you might even think you know just the right song
to bring satan's last stronghold quivering to its apologetic knees, but they also might laugh
at you hysterically, slit your throat in a joking manner, and bury you in the shade
of a bulletwood tree, mark it with a pile of dolphin bones, a place the tribespeople can visit
when the mood strikes for a good laugh, the best medicine
for whatever aspect of island life might be plaguing them, rest assured
that it won't be publicly-funded sports complexes, or the prices at whole foods, and those lines
there won't be any kind of lacking in community spirit, not on this small island
everyone here is living the same miracle, for it is their teamwork, it makes their dream work
it has their nine year olds hoping, and praying to the stars
that someone new might roll ashore fresh, a head to be impaled, a message to be left
watching the sun go up and down, a brand new statue of liberty
to lose over sadness to maggots, to the sands of time, bring us your tired, the head won't say
it won't ask for your poor, or all your huddled masses
bring them fucking no one, arrows for all your asses
whereas the coconuts, those you can leave, those can be left
and right there is good enough, that is plenty far enough

you can always tell when someone is counting backwards from ten
even if it sounds like noise, what-with certain looks coming from certain faces, articulated
boldly and without apology, no, the tiger people are not sorry
no one has to enamor that color palette, *denise*, no one has to like you
jeremy, you cannot make us, no one has to care about your thingamabobs, or the count
you want more? go find a ukulele, and then go find your truest selves to then go and fuck
vociferously, joust at the moon in your own backyard, but vociferously bring us the coconuts
is that too much to ask, really? to be left alone? on an island in the middle of the ocean?

THE BEAR PROBLEM

it was the air that moved, but no one else saw it
the dying song of the orcas
but no one else heard it, so you were afraid to ask

about the pattern, found in the ceiling texture
the scripture that softened in pink milk
kill yourself, it said, keep going
monday, followed by tuesday

an ego with moons, born as storms
a second grader asking the gym teacher about testicular cancer
can you imagine
the imagined power
of imagined secrets? of what is written on the napkins inside of that lunchbox?

it was muggsy bogues, the birds that flew into the window
birds whose broken beaks you prayed for, sobbing, that you stopped throwing in the dumpster
like they were red apple cores
and started throwing in the woods, like they were green apple cores
dead personalities rightful to a spiritual pasture, and with a rolodex, you hated yourself

it was the handjob
over a chocolate starfish, dynamic, ecological failure over a burning barrel
a soul that was sold for a charred sandwich
and what that meant for other people

whereas the forest, manifested
the treeline in focus, is death itself beaten
by a mindfulness technique
beaten to death, you are invited
but you can also stay here

but you do know it was the gorilla
you waved, and then it waved back
so you felt strange, and therefore alone
when enter sandman at virginia tech made you cry and cry and cry

in the jeans that you were wearing, and the shorts they became
who you became, a devil from tasmania
sobbing, and heaving
with not-good-enoughedness

when you heard what we heard
your people did not
and prayer was a boomerang

FOR THE DIRECTOR OF MUSIC

seated in the peace of two parkas, in the sunshine heat of a summertime forest, sweating
and smiling, the heyoka observes a deer, on approach to its reflection, seen dimly
in the clear riverbed, it is clearly seen, a soul pants for streams of water
it longs for a great mountain, floating in the western sky, as deep calls to deep

in the language of sacred clowns, visions of truth are delivered in the terror of storms
to the ashamed, to their all-consuming ache, which is the throb of yearning for light
while knowing a hard thing to know, rest is in the darkness
the words that live in falling water
they begin with the beating of a drum, with sticks grabbed in the cold wind, howling

the noise of eternity over silent land is heard, and then transcribed
from the ancestral thunderbirds
stand tomorrow, in the town square faithfully, in the afternoon heat of august, present yourself
as a mirror, wear a third parka, and beneath a bigger hat, sweat, shiver, and smile toothily

point at a one-footed goose, make mention of its fearsome hiss
for a cardinal will then swoop, explain the shock of its red wings
cutting through the aesthetic, skywriting with blood, emphasize mystery as a good friend
as a bird under consideration, fed, flapping, and flying to infinity, and beyond that, to florida
the bottom of the pain, the place where the olive leaf is found, and then presented
the message that is not clear, until it is made clear, until the nothingness is made into a new thing
and the twist is made fresh, presently the birds of thunder have again located
the snakes that rattle, whereupon they hurled themselves into canyons

a demise met in varying degrees of poof, poof, poof
deep having called to deep from the depths, and to the depths
when noise was heard through the great volume of silence, heat up the ice cubes, it said
for it is the best of both worlds, stupidity, which was hesitation confessed into humility

and knowledge, that birds are always perched, and paying attention, always ready
always wishing someone would fill in the blank, tell them that, say it until the season changes
back into darkness, say it walking backwards, again and again
all the way into the woodline, into the quick death of a wintertime sunset, wave goodbye
and wear not one parka, or even a t-shirt, but lather yourself generously in sunscreen
with a wider smile, wipe the sweat from your brow, make it funny, make it hilarious
you, you having been born to die twice, call that living

the wild punchline of a wild calling, the terror of the coming storm will be your happiness
in disguise, stick out your tongue, touch one nostril, make bad noises with your bad face
and go on with your bad self, bad to the bones made clean, in mortal agony, make good use
of the blessing of shame, make the people see themselves in your nonsense, in your bare ass
shove-up a broomstick, sweep-up a sidewalk, admonish inattention to detail
with a sign hung from your neck, boldly, say that your name is my name, too
and make for the treeline, at dusk, whistle to the anglo-saxons the tune of the jingleheimer

SHERMAN'S MARCH TO THE SACRAMENTO KINGS

the meek will be huddled to banjos, on the night of broken glass, there will be people
bulldozed hilariously as jokes, and steamrolled into the concrete as stains, as objects of blame
glowing as human torches, that will be interstate seventy-five northbound, peak foliage toledo
after the school choice homeschooling cash hits the electronics store fan, and then the needle
the consulting firms will convince the corporations to roll into public education
like it's gaza, armed to incentivize brand new thoughtless avenues
to a fresh crack in the sidewalk, go buy yourselves something nice, like an approved textbook
or a virtual reality headset, a pressure-cooked series of excuses to roll into downtown
on an inevitable monday, like it's gaza
now it's a throwback tuesday, so political prisoners are learning how few rooms are waiting
in the one true heaven, how there is no such thing as a political prisoner
please go back to your dreamless sleep
that is the tutelage of teeth, cut like swords, of jaws set with knives, men who are cunts
and women who are dicks, empirical descriptions far more sensible when used with the gender
reversed adorably, in classrooms with cute little drones, circling from above like cute little hawks
in such a world, what doesn't constitute trouble?
what happens to transsexuality slightly before, or just after, what always happens
to the people of color, the tradition that never graduates, the midnight train that gets here by noon the
firewood is still being gathered, open the books that remain, isaiah fifty-one, twenty-one
twenty-two, twenty-three, squiggle a line between crazy and plausible, take a stand
 between a neighbor and something bad, because they really tie the room together, do they not?
asking for friends, trying to save the sacramento kings, to locate the seminoles, we have to help
nebraska football, and the guadalajara boxing fans whispering about deportations
in the dollar general produce section, asking para hermanos mios, will they be okay?
briefly consider the inherent tension in how an avocado makes it way to brooklyn
tension must be out-dreamed, and out-cared, in order to live the same miracle
in order to get to where we are going, we are in need of some-something, please
awareness, maybe empathy, but probably not, so a common tongue, the catching
of a good-old fashioned passionate ass whoopin', shoes, coat, and hat tooken
confessions made under a pitcher of water, which means that #whipthathoass, pause, reads as
hashtag whip that ho ass, unpausing, among other clumsy forms of limited justice, fumbled
over bullies begging en route to an understanding, welcome to the black parade
to the greater douchebagery, that's right, less than fifty thousand dollars, say our fucking names
before we all die anyway, before we all go the way of the transexualsaurus rex
bitching and wondering, about apologies, about whether or not you can be both bat-shit bonkers
and still be right about something, the translation of crop circles, a penny flipped into a well
a blind squirrel, wild with mange, extrapolating with a cross-eyed seriousness

about the big ten, and belief, it says the cornhuskers are back, from the neighborhood bar, cried
having beaten purdue, that is the paranoia caused, and then exploited, by extroverts
in the hour of the underdog, as the climate migration is coming, is here, and it will be punished
ruthlessly after one disruption, resolved, that the pope of tomorrow is again going to read
a half-assed apology over a bag full of skulls, so what are we even talking about?
this is a discussion about precedent, and liberal gun ownership, denise, jeremy
and your lack thereof, subtle differences among fighting styles, the front foot, the back foot
detailed importance as to what might happen, when the bell rings dixie, imagine all of the people

COMPOUND FRACTURE

it was enough open bone
to grip with a closed fist, most stopped eating
a corn dog, and it was good
that no one poked the leg with a popsicle stick

for when your leg explodes
it is abrupt, how they slide you into the trunk of a car
and drive you to a temperature-controlled building
the sandwiches there, are cut diagonally
with precision, they are sold from vending machines

people do eat bones

many-several calcium bones

salted, it is the bone marrow
the crunch of human molar into dead bird
it is a certain cafeteria aloneness, not so great
the point gets lost

over pins and screws, holes made from drilling
and butterscotch pudding, it is now littered with crushed anti-inflammatories
that is excellent news

something happened that could not be withstood
the tough bone exploded
something happened that could not be withstood
a moment in time, a bomb

we were so sure of things
and then just like that

egg salad
egg salad sandwiches

THE LIVING DEAD BUFFALO

on broken concrete, it is fine
when the tailbone goes numb
when the onyx unfolds angrily above you, it formulates, it is plotting
the uncertainty meant to crawl
past the triune bones of the ear canal, at the end of act two

the fire will teach you to inhale painlessly
the years eaten by locusts, and all of that hatred, the constancy of threats, of panthers
dispatched, tree-to-tree behind you
that is fine, breathe-in the badness
with generosity, and resolve

that the feeling was real, you did not make it up
something was happening to the hopeful and tough
behold, for here is the new thing, open the narrow gate
sow carraway and scatter cumin, in quietness and trust
that is your strength, a threshing sledge, new and sharp, with many teeth
that is what you will be, before you spring into being

life will be announced
over a season of deep friendship, made with painful death
when suddenly the nothingness is primordial
and the anticipation is energizing, any minute now, like a triceratops
released from its stall, for there are streams rising in the wasteland

in the faraway pink and orange
of the ignition-turning sunrise over the golgotha
you can hear it, and you can feel it
the low rumble of cavalry
of the living dead buffalo, charging through the dust, out there in the distance, you can feel it
you can pay for my student loans

JEANNIE NEEDS A SHOOTER

she grew up scrubbing the walls of a chain-smoking north denver victorian, hot vinegar
over a hillside grid called childhood, over booze, over each other, they forgot she had a name
or had a future, when dad got caught talking on the phone with a woman in pueblo
mama turned herself into a sangria slush, and lived a broken soul's life, bouncing off cavestone
until it bumped into the stalagmites at gaetano's, her expiring martini smile at the end of the bar
laughing off the roadside discovery of her husband's bygone skull, a wet log rotting
as a little girl remembers, thinking about the only time he was ever impressed, it was a picture
of marlene dietrich and a musical saw, with feathers in her hair and soldiers clamoring for a wink
having turned down all kinds of nazi money, having made certain fans all the more certain
a little girl wanted to be worth noticing, worth anything to anyone who might learn her name
it was not six months after the murder, and there she was downtown under the lights
in a breezy dress, and wowing evening-goers with the halloween noises of a glimmering saw
hurting so much that she burned real heat, pushed real smoke into every crack of denver concrete
insisting she be discovered, she found work at gaetano's under a certain promise
and it never gets old, watching mama drink, watching the men there lean into her, unchecked
as deep mountain mafia, the undercurrent, the subtext of ongoing happenstance
it does not care how young the girl on her smoke break might be, should she bear witness
to something she shouldn't, poise needs to be the plan, tits perked and that smile wide
or they said mama would go just like daddy did, desperately begging to sodomize them all
they said, if she told anyone, they would know, if there was any change in anything
there was a special place in the mountains where cougars and wolves expected bloodshed
so truth was bent like the saw, as if life itself now depended on strange noises
she was under management, and made to smile, to pose for advertisements, to exceed tiredness
of denver surgical tools, nineteen fifty-three, look at this blonde with a talent for music, folks
ain't she sharp? she'll come by all the tables, and you can see where she gets it from
right over there, and that empty glass would wave, and then bonk her head on a lighting fixture
leaving her daughter, to be shot with glares, from the shadows underneath the fedoras
it was a list of names, menu-holders that she could not shake from her legs, and it was torment
fake life under fake lighting, face covered in smoke grease and mama slumped-over, drooling
it moved consciousness past the survival instinct, and pushed her through a portal, a woomf
sound made upon the realization that she was living-out an expression, her back against the wall
stuck to a green leather stool, behind that podium, what was living? would it only ever amount
to this undersized bra that never came off? a dead end, the one dream that had presented itself
the dream that denverites might care enough to learn who she was, just as her father had fawned
over marlene, it was small thinking, and fruitless, stardom compared with giant stardom's
immediate collapse against the wall, a leopardess must go for the throat, and rip it out, step on it
standing there in a downtown stillness, a claw tapping on the window glass of bighorn firearms

she imagined an armament befitting to a black hole, and in her reflection was a brand new dream
mama didn't know it yet, but tonight was last call, so a young girl asked which two
of what she was looking at didn't kick as bad as the others? and which two
of these knives might the storehand use on an elk? and what's he doing later, by the way?
what's it like talking about guns all the time? maybe your thing could become my thing, she said
and that could be our thing, la cosa nostra, got herself a deal and asked for a cigarette
stepped out into the sunset braless over the cold sidewalk that she found herself motherfucking
en route to the event horizon, furious, cocked and loaded, tits-out ready to make sauce

CHIMP SIXTY-FIVE

from the rare bird farm
in miami florida
ham the chimpanzee, monkey number sixty-five
was taken, taught to push buttons
with electric shocks
and banana pellets
he was launched into space
he did the strange work
he endured a malfunction
and rocketed into the ocean
he was okay, having landed violently
this constellation monkey
made to do that
he lived to see more things
chronic heart disease, chronic liver disease
we buried his skeleton in maryland
his chimpanzee guts found some of the orange dirt in new mexico
in the ground
ham was given two holes in which to dream
about life and afterlife, both torn apart
ideally on his way to forgetting most of it
ham now rides on a flying carpet
ham can show you the world
dying, whimpering, ended
it let its heart contrive
it opened a box of lies, took wonder by wonder
over, sideways, and under
the table, a whole new mortal coil
a poisonous cauldron of stew, in which the russians used a dog
no es bueno guadalupe
it's not great bob
these kids are going to kill it as adults
and kill unilaterally, if you can believe it
they are going to blame us for the unilateral killing
total foghorn
the end of our favorite show
a charbroiled thickburger, they will say

they will try to say, for nothing is ever over
until everything becomes nothing worth muckduck, absolutely

ADRENOCHROME BACCHANALIA

those are hearts filled with rainforest gold
those proclaimed lives of sin, those you contemplate as cannon fodder
you whose slumber is drink, whose dreams are masturbation, whose life is darkness
poured through the eyes, you, you pointing, a double portion of your own cup
per your own request, you dog, your own vomit
having paid no mind at all to the roadkill, no, not one condescending recital
hissed through your folded hands
was made in the heartfelt hope of a smaller hellscape, it was about you, and yours
the beverage was adrenochrome, the sin was a rimjob, your prayers were a bonfire
fed, and crackling, warmth for the fingers and the toes on a cold night, wondering
how can we have some more of nothing? you shrugged, mouths stuffed
with blackened marshmallows, you chewed and chewed and chewed, and then you swallowed
fuck 'em, you said
through graham cracker, spitting the inferno
we don't negotiate with terrorists, you explained
grace having been set aside by grace from houston
and her husband michael, theirs will be a gnashing of invisaligns
resolved, fuck 'em, are we saying that right? just kidding, just condescending, just like you
hell being a place on earth, just up the driveway, just north of houston
the brimstone conversation is a sodomy playlist
an exact type of people, they put snipers in helicopters above the park
to protect sport utility vehicles from mother nature
they point at the lobster tank
fog up the glass, draw hapless little hearts around helpless little prey, lustful
over its final moments as witness to a microwave door
closing loudly on a stick of butter
resolved, let the wilderness and its towns raise their voices
let them imagine trying to lasso the moon, let them imagine shooting it out of the sky
these are choices, indeed, there is a church in the wild
the pastors like fubu, the deacons wear timberlands
and the allied congregation, is armed with american eagles, and privileged access
marshall who is not mellow, melinda who is upset
about what is happening to jamiroquai, who is white, melinda who is still learning
how to turn stone-faced, in the direction of her own color palette, unyielding
a forehead harder than flint, be not dismayed, though they are a rebellious house
fear not, for they will come to us, the highways and the hedges
they have never been here, allow us to learn only specific things from stonewall jackson

to take advantage of the terrain,
who are these philistines, that they should defy the armies of the Living God?
the paw of the bear
get these bitches out into the ontological gap, wide open, make them have to trust one another
in the darkness, and see each other in the daylight, they should win, should being the operative
against a regiment armed only with whispers, frankincense, and only misunderstood as only
until the queen of the south rises, the woman with purple feet
the vintage having been trampled, this will be tough to understand, the party She intends

JOY IN MUDVILLE

a flat-rolled american shorthair glows freshly dead
under the iridescent shine of the perkins by the highway

mangled, without meowing and reimagined by the noise
of a truck, en route to a text message with pills

pork rinds, pineapple blunts, and bacardi one-fifty-one
salamanders with explicit plans to cumsoak, stipulated

and resolved, a white bottle of lighter fluid
turns a black woodline orange, for it is their cove, shared under the stars

with fireworks, stolen from the highway barn
warm in the face, the noise of it all is giggled-at, fuck is said between hiccups

over warm rants, what their parents believe
warmly, which is dixie piled-upon with jagermeister from dixie cups, piling

pulling, forgetting to pray, praying to forget
that salamanders can make more salamanders while the barn owls hoot

TREE IN THE RAIN

it was long after nightfall, 'neath a tree located and secured in the hard rain
high above the bloody pond, the hornet's nest, and the peach orchard, as the bad noise of pigs
ripped through the dead, likewise the wounded remained in the confederate mud, toiling
those whose fates were realized under rototillers, and regrettably could not be hastened
by pleading with the moonlight, nothing came of those wild prayers
as wild boar, opportunistically, made wild martyrs out of broken, ingestible bonemeal
belief survived, all night between the thunderous and incessant foghorn cannons firing
from the river, as the timed explosions bombarded the need for sleep, belief remained
through the incendiary lights, as good luck meant getting to see that which unfolded
in the rainfall, in the cold down-below, where the lives of the hard-living
were yet again made to live through destiny eating them alive, and en masse
those who had sang Jesus, lover of my soul, whose brothers were singing it still, onward
and with intention through tears, crackers, and uncooked meat, unwilling to risk a fire
during a detailed rest, what respite meant specifically after a day spent dealing
with an early morning volcano, which bled lava into a long night on the tennessee river
and into an important daybreak, in which someone who shouldn't, but did so anyway
had to believe fiercely, a man who earlier that day stood next to a close friend
as he lost his head to a cannonball, as the skull was gone, and the menace kept rolling, it galloped
over to a set of nearby legs, and it took those too
meaning that leadership sometimes means that your overcoat must sometimes carry little bits
of brain from one important moment to the next, because if that man believes
then everyone believes, and will give their fingernails to the cause of the night, clawing
towards counterattack, hope being hopelessness ignored, the pigs being a loud population
over which to pray, forward-still was the position held by the man 'neath the tree in the rain
hat brimmed low and dripping, seated on a rock with a knife through an apple
resolved, when even the bravest of the brave, and the meanest of the mean, were nervous
and held onto doubt, and wanted to know what the man in the raindrops was thinking
could he not hear the oinking, and the screaming, consistent through the intermittent explosions?
had we all not bore the devil's very own day?
yes, he said, but we're going to lick them tomorrow, and send all of their bumfuck legacies back
down the tennessee river apologizing, for when asked about preparations for retreat
the question drew a quick retort, an angry proposition to the opposite thinking, an attack
to be made at daylight, having not yet despaired of kicking antebellum from its asshole crying
one day spent on the backfoot, it was altogether one too many, and therefore never again
all of this, never again, as the enemy was meant to be trampled by reinforcements, and history
made into a stain, and so it was, and so it is, a stain, a lingering kaboom
you should puke, go take a stroll through the american hallway of inconvenient echoes

the hogs quarreling over a carnival feast, the feral raid launched into the arm-and-leg pile
adjacent to the hospital tent, there was the grunting, there was the rooting in the human remains
freedom having again been won, freedom having again been maintained, brutally
by those who were devoured, and then digested, those who were defecated in the morning steam
gave roaring life to pollinating flowers, and to fruit-bearing trees
here is to the lost heroes, who returned as forgotten roots
and made everything new, for a while, for a price, the dead having again purchased nothing

DECEPTION PASS

fumbling with feng shui coins, chinese dreamers in burlap sacks
tried to smell the douglas firs of washington, and focus on stillness, on the afterlife
after the inspection of agents, armed with explicit orders, lawful exclusion
and neon justice, this custom of souls unceremoniously thrown to the orcas
bones picked clean from deception pass to dead man's bay, as fresh skeletons
became forgotten chinese-american hopefuls, a currency unto themselves, a campfire
that was signaled, or not signaled, from strawberry island
before the tight currents ran fast into the whirlpools, it was all darkness
to approaching captains, needlings of knowing the darkness
news pertinent also to the huddled poor, a state of knee-hugging abuzz over gold mountains
and gig harbor canneries, the limbs they could stand to lose
to the railroads, to the mines, if the whales did not eat you
such outcomes were chinese gravy, or fireworks sold on the fourth of july
as one little nugget meant one new house, come what gossip may
to the gold mountain wives of the homeland, women whose husbands were shuffled
onto boats by opium wars, shuffled into the strait of juan de fuca, and the angry chop
of the salish sea, into the guiding hands of postwar confederate captains
resolved, unwilling to participate in a negotiated peace, not so much
no thank you, came way out here to shoot bald eagles in-flight
and to haggle over polished canoes, and with confidence, and with cash
as chinese run five hundred bucks per head that nods politely
and guts every fish you throw at them, without disagreement, and without much weight
facelessly they hopped into a cross section of people at sea, co-animals, unafraid
of drowning underwater, contextualized by the continuation of drowning above it
the bulldozer fear, of losing forever
as prisoners to the puget sound, helpless, which is the common timpani roll, the cold sushi
of shared incompetence cannot fight the moonlight, or anything forever
even if it feels like you can, even if you're like that
and the dream feels so real, and so right in front of you, that you will die trying
to pass through the angriest of saltwater, through the whirlpools that do not care
and the orcas that do not know your name, but it was all whatever, a simple, and universal whatever
what-with certain problems having just the one answer
and what that has to mean, so much fun wrapped-up in seaweed, inside the sensory reality
of a burlap sack, hairs plucked nervously from each forearm
high above the thrashing water of the salish sea at night, there goes nothing, breathing
and betting the farm on black, a primordial occurrence

prayers for darkness tailing the devil in a lifeboat, there goes something
sighing, what light from yonder island burns? it is the beast
and destiny the skeleton, a box that is checked, or a retreat from bad luck under an envious moon

CONSTELLATIONS OF THE SOUTH

in the winds of an alabama shoreline, in the chiling waters
of its early may disposition, a child is already half-knowingly in the waves
of its conviction, fresh with the idea of himself, once more unto the breach
he will again, and again, proceed, as with the shooting end pointed north
indeed he pulled the trigger, for he openly rebelled, and then crawled
through the wild pigs, through the open guts of his old friends
was his open and bloodletting, cotton-eyed soul, as it could somehow remain
it rescued-then a fallen eagle of that same blackened field, and with a broken leg
to match his infected-own, so it was, whereupon these new companions
of echoing battle limped away together, and escaped
the dead-livestock territories of all that cumbersome noise, decimated
into a very small fire, a very simple heat, a nation of two having forged together
a glowing-fluorescent and death-knowing bond, a broken man, a wounded eagle
a life content-now over breathing in the vicissitudes
of organic silence, general health, and the unlonely crackle of a shared campsite okayness
in hiding, for there is more than one way to age
and this one had stolen butter, a journal
of complicated soup, and a most odd understanding
mutual alongside that onward-limping, and yet forward-leaning eagle
as time found its way through the forest, the death rattle of this pairing's incendiary baggage
softened, and the pause felt permanent, so together the two of them recollected
their respective wingspans, purchased for themselves two tickets
to the auburn football game, and as a team they felt empowered
beyond indifferent, having taken their seats in the losing stands, quietly perched
while the war bled loudly over the emotional gridlock, and the unsuccessful passing of time
on third down, for they had forgotten themselves, witnessed the warring eagle
opening wide, when off it soared, circling with spectacle high-above, and all the way around
the stadium, and the playing field itself, that is how you animal
it showcased its talons, it modeled its thunderous wings
and screamed into the souls
of the auburn faithful, all of the losers who in remembering themselves
made-way for a tiger's roaring victory, chiseled there in strip'd lore
having disproved the insurmountable, the miracle of it
then growled with thirst, and demanded that something die, whereupon once again the eagle
raised a wing in willing sacrifice, and flew boldly into the shining sun
slowly, when the bird then retreated, for the bird had already lost
smiling over a paradoxical calm, over the truth cut into pieces, reassembled

so having then dove beak-first into the open fields of history
screaming, in remembrance of the war eagle, crying, to please also remember
his very good friend, and the life they found together
in otherwise broken places, for it was necessary, and it became lovely
all of those painful nights endured lost under the mystery of stars, healing
and debilitated, tracing-together the dots that connected the bear
to the constellations of the south, to the open sky that poured-forth hints to a greatness
that glowed in the darkness, hovering-over the loud voices, where a violent future was real

MOUNTAIN IN THE WESTERN SKY

no front bumper remained
on the dirt-white nissan versa
teeth knocked out
colored wires hanging, and dragging
making all kinds of bad noise
down cleveland avenue, little palestinian flags
opposite the star of david
a standoff between the walgreens and the taco bell
many lanes of traffic
observed, a broken car on broken concrete, a broken driver, easing the wheel
into a recollection of saint phillip
and saint peter, crucified upside down
can't help thinking about an early sunrise
bug is aware of windshield, of rex teeth hammered through bone
but still, tell the nissan versa all about tomorrow, the possible shades
of both pink and orange
that will speak new things into the cold air
wow, came fresh-back to odd senses, upside-down
remembering, do not care
what happens encompassing the watermelon
of what happens to the nissan versa
juxtaposed by incendiary faith, worn like brass knuckles
welded into the hands, into the very being, those rex teeth only tighten the soulfire grip
of wonderment, for what is all of this
compared to the belief held in tomorrow?
an explanation of this perspective began, a final brimstone sermon unpunctuated
abruptly the television flickered-off
came-to in a forest, parked at the gate
with the trees pointing skyward
over gig harbor, port orchard, belfair and key peninsula
nobody is ever going back to that half-smiling midsize
nobody is ever looking away from the mountain in the western sky

SQUARE PEG, SQUARE HOLE

the plumber harvested his destiny from behind the church wall
clumsily, having broken-loose the closet, when out fell a skeleton above questioning
and under renovation, there was a revelation, an accident, a square peg for a square hole
as it was a coincidence, sorry, it was providential
that he found the exact same amount of money
stolen from the church eight years earlier, wow, the genius of that, this random criminal
hiding his loot where no one would look, where he-himself, hypothetically, could not look
a place where the money would neither grow, nor spend, how dastardly, downright brilliant
and unsurprising, how altogether unfortunate are the sons of eli
because if cents could help make sense out of the sin
the insurance claim would smother the quote-unquote problem with a blanket
and double the money they started with, which is the victimhood of various legalities
being followed to the letter, and then followed-up, of course, naturally and thoroughly
by a media that does its job, in a town that really cares, communicates
its disinterest, in that it yawned when the investigation was shut down, inconclusively
punctuated by a donation to the crime stoppers program
they probably got to write that off too, these people and their prosperity gospel
a gnat strained-out to swallow a camel, his, a net worth of one-hundred million dollars
but no, he will not take a salary, this, what is the word, *personality*
he who must not be named, he who had no room at the inn, no room at the basketball arena
for the hurricane victims
it was inaccessible, they said, *fartknocker*
the floors are a bit wet, because the floors are always a bit wet, always inaccessible
that whitewashed tomb filled with storytelling bones, with emphasis placed on both white
and washed, that has-been, that never-was, that *videographer* whose efforts were *honored*
by proclamation from the city, because that is the world we live in
people eat shit and die, people receive two-point-five times the amount
of covid funding necessary from the sax player, the sex-check protection program, abused
to the benefit of the sometimes hurricane protection shelter, once they are good and ready
on the maginot line of door greeters, the extroverted centipede, crisply-pleated
so please use the red carpets, to wipe-off your plebeian shoes, please, before you enter
such a golden sanctuary, and its bless'd shine, please allow one of our polished jackals
flashing you a plastic smile, to take your tattered coat
and share with you a battered chuckle, this crazy weather we've been having
that is a sense of humor, get ready to laugh
et ready to rock, we locked a drummer inside of a plastic cage
and by special request, we prayerfully splurged on a reverential smoke machine

so this is a big day, the band is really excited
about the songs they have been electrifying, away in a manger, are you kidding?
you are going, to piss your khaki pants, we are going, to ask you to leave, but hey
we really do get it, selah, so maybe next time, of course we understand
because that is just what we do around here
we empathize religiously

TEACH GRANDPA TO SUCK THE EGGS

each shade of orange plays its part, a color palette to a broken name
neatly swept into a pile of glass shard
eggs having been scrambled in bacon grease, and peppered, the breeze is now spoken to
in the driveway, big bet, these brainwave bombardiers, these talks with an empty kitchen's
running faucet, it's giving decline, keeping that same limited energy
in and out of denial, muckduck over a thursday
today's variation of yesterday, established ahead of tomorrow's review
furiously, frustration as a broken record, the four-by-six flash cards
meant for dead beggars, flashing
for unseen comets on a friday, in love and unbridled
there went a mountain ram, unburdened unto the breach and foaming with hellos
from the box, quoting the book of malachi from a tilted alignment, fuck him, he said
the taco bell parking lot
resolved, a peacemaker
falling to the ground in pieces
remembering to flash a smile, a weightlessness
under orion's nebula, a thud that was made in the grass, again and again and again
a general awareness, dying plants
browning ferns hung from the back patio over an unfamiliar scrapbook left open
a sea of tranquility with flickering sunrises, fading sunsets, and forgotten pleasantries
a general numbness to salt water taffy, where are my manners?
what was that morning on the oregon coast?
that chinese takeout, what was that promenade evening in the sugary air?
the very beginning of seeing things, phantom threads introduced
as mannequins, moving between headaches in the sunshine
over soups to forget
the years that can still be pieced together with laughs
which is a big pill, losing, that is
saying goodbye, swallowing, sitting there like you always have
breathing in and out, shitting in a bag and sucking down veggie burgers through a paper straw
humbled, hello and proceed bravely, tell me again about tomorrow
do not stop until the horizon sends an army, as it will take an army
or this lamp will burn ferociously onward, as weird as it ever was
peering forward dimly, as in a mirror, through the glaze, through the glass
fawning over endlessness
long after the last bat leaves the belltower
prior to relegation, prior to promotion

from drooling fondly
'neath the brim of this hat, there will be an idea, if do this be the end
farewell cried the wounded piper boy
methinks me breathes me last me fears, from whence came these celestial brothers?
two people united for an instant, resolved, and resting peacefully, the alien crumbled
but he felt alright, he loved it, in those exact final words
he loved it all, it being a tornado, a turquoise light
beckoning with solsbury hill, brisket sliders, and banter under the redwoods, strolling

HARMONICA ROADS

arteries of a concrete valley
pool their rainwater
into a wet pile of snakes
en concierto, cut-shadowed by orange fences, overrun with ivy
living, dying

ongoing same as anywhere
cheap and confused
this is our soup, that is our pizza, here is the oxidation

soot that we rub on our chest
please close your eyes, and then spin, and then point
ask that pez dispenser
exactly how they have been marginalized, and then they will tell you, and then you will tell them
that you have a gun

that the password taint gooch
which is a hint, for it had been unchanged, for too long
for sure, for the shire
is life up its own ass

you roll along long enough, tires on the same trails
and the journey lives itself without you

knowing you can't unknow something that you know you already know
'cause that means whispering to yourself
real quiet, over and over
that you never knew it at all
until the shame goes numb

twenty-three over the limit only felt like eight, lost in bad thoughts
got to bad thinking, the journey is all there is

you know this hunk of metal will do whatever your right foot tells it to
take you anywhere you might want to live, and maybe die
what-with mysteries still unfolding, and being what they are

while mercy remains new with each morning
should the undead rise
smack themselves around a bit, and hunger-onward in a forced reality
built on more than a feeling, imagination being a concrete mixer
a determination to find what isn't there
a zipper, hidden in the atmosphere, open-up that bitch like told you so

MUSKETS FOR THE BEAR PROBLEM

albert bierstadt's last of the buffalo
albert bierstadt's sunrise on the matterhorn
that rose over mackinac island, the wolves of west palm beach, absolutely
a rolling pebble, in an empty chamber
called pictured rocks, the shoreline dunes of sleeping bear michigan

rejoice with other hands trembling, disney quest orlando
and lake superior, clinging to muskets for the awakening bear problem
ahead of a deciduous breach
darkwing ducks as gunsmoke fades
and silence wins, once more
call being lost a good thing, a cheeseburger in paradise

having thunderstruck boston's more than a feeling
boston's peace of mind whilst the muskets cracked, and the ramparts fell
to rest over bottles of thunderbird
empty corpses, those whom others thought they were inherently better-than
bostonian, alone-together cadavers hugging the grass
in a pause, in an appearance

that of a rotting jack-o-lantern, the deathly taste of fortified wine
means that death itself can no longer be tasted

how's it sold? good and cold
what's the jive? the bird's alive
what's the price? thirty twice, or free on skid row

as unopened crates, as faux-generosity
meant to push endurance into a purpose
beyond stardust, beyond cigarettes, survival with luster
for those without sixty cents, and the rich folk a mile away

fear becomes food
death, a source of energy
and a place to live, no more freezing, no more flying away
the sword of job hath been unsheathed from orion's nebula
and the time has come for an updated charter
big-enough signatures, the bear needs to see
that little engines can be strainlessly found, as they drew a map next to fuck you

found, yes, disarmed, not so much
for we are a glowing problem, and that is neon purple ink, drying on a legal document
deez nutz, jeremy, the treeline will not be surrendered
lost, denise, but not surrendered
an outcome is an owl's own hooting perspective

THE MOON IS ORANGE

purpling was the sky over ecola point
between gulps of mexican beer, the planet was unrecognizable
to a dangling studebaker
it was consistency overruled, that a good word for the wrong noun
held meaning
it was granulated sugar
a most breathable, late september air
released in surrender, that was appomattox
over a pause, a moment to feel the armistice, a breeze
after the wind let go
it gathered itself into a fist, positioned itself for a bump
of plainspoken benevolence, unpredictably meek
was a flat palm's relenting
from a flat palm's downward-pressing
on the thrash-about skull of a tasmanian devil, the stillness was strange
era strano en italiano, life feeling blameless, the actualization of a ventriloquist dummy
as blood flowed to spinal cord, the pain warmed into a quiet snooze
a froggered happiness, having danced in the headlights with guns
in honor of a charcoaled falcon's broken wing, roadkill feathers
of a bygone speed pointing skyward, beautifully
he would remember those fish tacos, he decided, blackened mahi mahi
and baseball games that chirped like crickets, how the lime in the beer made bubbles
against the inertia
upright, there he was
the target remained
at peace with the waves, and in love with the waves
sighing, because it was an actual chance to sigh, that was a warm sidewalk, wasn't it?
a warm life settled, sometimes hard
to sometimes remember
how gentle the passing moments can be, when the moon turns orange
and jupiter appears next to it
you do not feel insane, changing the tense when you are alone
but do not feel that way, a Planet-Sized Space Monster
places its enormous hand on your paralyzed back
with sincerity, the mystery colored over the horizon line
on a beach with tranquil scars
dolphins are jumping over music, and the killer whales can hear it

something in the quiet purr
of a tide's backward roll, over the pebbles and the sand
you are not crazy
says one of the voices

you are okay
you are okay
you are okay

a mostly respectful, mostly grateful acknowledgment
of influence, in some particular order

The Triune God, biblical prophets and scribes, marissa and other family, cardi b
vin diesel, jimmy buffett, dr. seuss, bruce springsteen and the e street band, pete maravich
my chemical romance, william shakespeare, thunderbird wine, technotronic, albert bierstadt
matt berninger and the national, brian fallon and the gaslight anthem, jack antonoff and bleachers
boston, pliny the younger, ac/dc, bill simmons, ryen russillo, zach lowe, cousin sal
june diane raphael, jason mantzoukas, paul scheer, dwight eisenhower, tupac shakur
warren zevon, kurt vonnegut, dr. hunter s thompson, 1883, eminem, the revenant, the blues brothers
the big lebowski, grand budapest hotel, rookie of the year, the killers, william carlos williams
donald ray pollock, reginald dwayne betts, peter gabriel, muggsy bogues
fascism, stonewall jackson, disney
john hancock

andrew whitmer is a writer from youngstown, ohio
extremely grateful, and with endless love, to God, his family, his friends
and to a willing readership, so many apologies
and a special thank you, also, to cathexis northwest press, for belief
and patience, thank you one thousand times
works of bad, early-life short fiction appeared in the three rivers review, jenny, and blood lotus
muskets for the bear problem is a debut of both form and full-length publication
with eternal sincerity, again
thank you all very much

Also Available from Cathexis Northwest Press:

Something To Cry About
by Robert T. Krantz

Suburban Hermeneutics
by Ian Cappelli

God's Love Is Very Busy
by David Seung

that one time we were almost people
by Christian Czaniecki

Fever Dream/Take Heart
by Valyntina Grenier

The Book of Night & Waking
by Clif Mason

Dead Birds of New Zealand
by Christian Czaniecki

The Weathering of Igneous Rockforms in High-Altitude Riparian Environments
by John Belk

If A Fish
by George Burns

How to Draw a Blank
by Collin Van Son

En Route
by Jesse Wolfe

sky bright psalms
by Temple Cone

Moonbird
by Henry G. Stanton

southern athiest. oh, honey
by d. e. fulford

Bruises, Birthmarks & Other Calamities
by Nadine Klassen

Wanted: Comedy, Addicts
by AR Dugan

They Curve Like Snakes
by David Alexander McFarland

the catalog of daily fears
by Beth Dufford

Shops Close Too Early
by Josh Feit

Vanity Unfair and Other Poems
by Robert Eugene Rubino

Destructive Heresies
by Milo E. Gorgevska

Bodies of Separation
by Chim Sher Ting

The Night with James Dean and Other Prose Poems
by Allison A. deFreese

About Time
by Julie Benesh

Suspended
by Ellen White Rook

The Unempty Spaces Between
by Louis Efron

Quomodo probatur in conflatorio
by Nick Roberts

Suspended
by Ellen White Rook

Call Me Not Ishmael but the Sea
by J. Martin Daughtry

Wild Evolution
by Naomi Leimsider

Coming To Terms
by Peter Sagnella

Acta
by Patrick Wilcox

Honeymoon Shoes
by Valyntina Grenier

Practising Ascending
by Nadine Hitchiner

Home Visit
by Michal Rubin

LA CIUDAD EN TI: THE CITY WITHIN YOU
by Karla Marrufo
Translated from the Spanish by Allison A. deFreese

<u>Resin in the Milky Way</u>
by Amanda Rabaduex

<u>Bone Hunting</u>
by Trinity Catlin

<u>Rabbit Hole</u>
by Crystal Ignatowski

<u>Self-Portraits as a Reddening Sky</u>
by Samuel Gilpin

<u>Desert</u>
by Eric Larsh

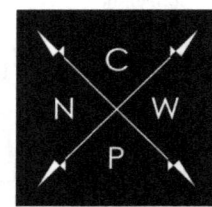

Cathexis Northwest Press

www.ingramcontent.com/pod-product-compliance
Lightning Source LLC
Chambersburg PA
CBHW081432070526
44586CB00020B/2560